M000010352

March
ON WASHINGTON

Written by
Douglas M. Rife

Good Apple
A Division of Frank Schaffer Publications, Inc.

Acknowledgment

I would like to thank John J. Oliver, Jr., CEO and Publisher of the *Afro-American Newspapers* for his generous permission to let us reprint materials from the pages of the *Richmond Afro-American*.

Editors: Christine Hood, Kristin Eclov,
        Deborah Ross Klingsporn
Illustration: Ron Lipking
Cover Illustration: Barbara Kiwak
Cover Design and Art Direction: Jonathan Wu
Inside Design: Anthony D. Paular
Graphic Artist: Randy Shinsato

GOOD APPLE
A Division of Frank Schaffer Publications, Inc.
23740 Hawthorne Boulevard
Torrance, CA 90505

GA131694

Contents

History in the Headlines Series

Surveys taken in the mid-1980s made famous the fact that American students do not like history, often ranking it as their least favorite school subject. Even tough subjects such as math were ranked higher because students saw them as more relevant than history.

Unfortunately, history has attained the reputation for being dull. Part of the reason students find history boring is that, for the most part, history textbooks tend to be lifeless, bland, and uninteresting—little more than a chronological recitation of events. A long litany of what happened when, where, and with whom conveys little of the human drama that makes history a rich and colorful story.

This is not to place the blame solely on textbook companies. The development of a textbook is a long and arduous process. Textbooks are generally written by editorial committees to please curriculum adoption committees—a sure recipe for a boring book. Textbooks also rely heavily on secondary sources, which are twice removed from original accounts. Most textbooks include few primary source materials. The student is rarely introduced to firsthand accounts such as letters, diaries, newspaper articles, songs, photographs, and speeches. The text loses its narrative flow and students never get a sense of history as a great *story,* which is, after all, the root word of *history.*

History taught in this way tends not to be remembered at all. When queried, the average American student has difficulty placing events such as the American Revolution and the Civil War in the correct decade in which they occurred.

The History in the Headlines series has a two-fold purpose. The first is to focus on seminal events—those that changed the very course of American history, such as the March on Washington during the hot days of August in 1963. It is clear that the speech of Martin Luther King, Jr., is one of the great speeches in American history, and that King's leadership changed America for the better—and for all time.

King is in the pantheon of great speakers in American history. The power of his language, his rhetorical skills, his imagery, and his moral convictions gave him and his message monumental force. His personality and his leadership skills to effect change are evident by historic legislation—the Civil Rights Act of 1964, the Voting Rights Act of 1965, and the Civil Rights Act of 1968—that was later passed, all of which alluded to his speech.

Secondly, the series gives students an opportunity to read primary source material—a newspaper account, an excerpt from King's "I Have a Dream" speech, editorial cartoons, and gospel songs celebrated at the march. The details surrounding the March on Washington are retold in compelling prose in newspaper accounts of the day. (Note: All handouts in this book are reproductions of actual documents. They have been printed in their original form to maintain their integrity. Any errors you may find are as they appeared in the original documents.)

Overall, the History in the Headlines series puts flesh on the skeletal histories found in basal textbooks. I hope you find it a useful supplement to your history curriculum.

The Newspaper As a Primary Source

"A newspaper is the history for one day of the world in which we live. . . ."

—George Horne

A newspaper is a snapshot of current events on a given day in history. A newspaper can be viewed as a rough draft of history and an important primary source of that information.

Students should note, however, that not all early newspaper reports are accurate. One of the most famous examples of an embarrassing mistake is the *Chicago Daily Tribune*'s coverage of the 1948 presidential election. Based on early returns, the newspaper printed a giant banner headline on the front page that read *DEWEY DEFEATS TRUMAN*. Of course, Truman actually defeated Dewey in 1948, winning 304 electoral votes to Dewey's 189. (The popular vote was 24,105,695 to 21,969,170.) If a historian were only to focus on that one newspaper as the source of information in researching the 1948 election, he or she would come to many false conclusions, to say the least.

Like all primary sources, a newspaper story should be read with a critical eye and attention to detail. Good historians check other sources of information to corroborate facts and check the authenticity and veracity of a particular source. Historians should try to understand the motives, if any, behind the manner in which a given event is covered.

This series allows students to investigate the newspaper as a primary source of information. Students will read contemporary accounts of historical events with fresh eyes, just as the original readers did on the day the story unfolded. This series also provides students with a taste of the drama surrounding the great seminal events in American history. Finally, this series will help students read current newspapers more critically by reminding them to question and analyze what they read in these first drafts of history.

Unit Overview and Objectives

	Objectives	Critical Thinking	Activities
Richmond Afro-American: "**Vast Sea of Humanity Raises Cry for 'Freedom'**"	• Analyze the reasons behind the March on Washington • Understand the basic elements of a newspaper story • Discover the five W's and how and inverted pyramid styles of journalistic writing • Understand the concept of primary source material	• Analyze a primary source document • Evaluate the important facts in a news story • Analyze data tables	• Read for comprehension • Rewrite a news story using the inverted pyramid • Identify the five W's and how in a story • Identify important leaders in the civil rights movement • Use data tables to answer questions and make conclusions
A Speech by Martin Luther King, Jr.: "I Have a Dream"	• Understand the impact and significance of the speech	• Analyze the speech for references, facts and strategy	• Answer questions and develop conclusions about the speech
Editorial Cartoons	• Understand pictorial symbolism used in editorial cartoons • Recognize the use of humor and stereotypes in editorial cartoons • Identify and judge a cartoonist's message and point of view	• Evaluate an editorial cartoon and form an opinion about the cartoonist's message	• Identify symbolism and strategies used in editorial cartoons • Restate an editorial cartoon's message in own words
Literature Connection: "The Battle Hymn of the Republic" "Free at Last"	• Understand songs as primary source material • Interpret symbolism used in songs	• Analyze songs for meaning and symbolism	• Read, listen to, and sing historical anthems • Answer questions regarding the songs' historical significance

Richmond Afro-American

"Vast Sea of Humanity Raises Cry for 'Freedom'"

Objectives

- Analyze the reasons behind the March on Washington
- Understand the basic elements of a newspaper story
- Discover the five W's and how and inverted pyramid styles of journalistic writing
- Understand the concept of primary source material

Vocabulary

Civil Rights: Rights guaranteed to U.S. citizens by the 13th, 14th, and 19th amendments to the Constitution, especially the right to vote and equal treatment under the law

Colored: A term once used to refer to people with skin color other than white. This term, though commonly used in the 1960s, is no longer considered proper.

CORE: The Congress of Racial Equality, a group of concerned citizens dedicated to seeing that all people, regardless of race, be treated equally; founded in 1942

Dixie: Refers to the southern states of the United States

Jim Crow: Laws passed to discriminate against African Americans

Recalcitrant: Refusing to obey; stubborn in opposition

Segregation: To isolate or separate, especially by racial groupings

Who's Who

Asa Philip Randolph (1889–1979)

Randolph was the organizer and moving force behind the March on Washington in 1963. Randolph had long been a leader in the civil rights movement from the 1920s. He first became active in the labor movement by founding the Brotherhood of Sleeping Car Porters, with the goal of obtaining fair wages and labor practices for black workers. Randolph first proposed a great March on Washington as early as 1941, while Franklin Roosevelt was president. To avert the march, Roosevelt established the Fair Employment Practices Commission.

William T. Sherman

Union general whose march through the South cut a swath of destruction.

Background

The Five W's and How/Inverted Pyramid Journalistic Writing Styles

In newspaper writing, the philosophy is to get the most important information in the lead paragraph of the story. This journalistic form of writing, called the **inverted pyramid**, was popularized in newspapers in the 1920s: The **lead** carries the most important information. The theory is that many people never read past the first paragraph, so it should carry the most important facts. The **middle paragraphs** carry important supporting information; the **ending paragraphs** also support the story, but could be cut if the story runs long. Good news stories also answer questions readers need to know—*who, what, when, where, why,* and *how.* These elements are called the **five W's and how**.

The following article is about the March on Washington, which was held on August 28, 1963. This March highlighted the country's need for civil rights legislation guaranteeing all Americans equal treatment under the law. It was during this March that Dr. Martin Luther King, Jr., gave the most notable speech advocating civil rights legislation and equality for blacks in all American history. His stirring rhetoric moved many in the audience to tears.

Suggested Lesson Plan

1. Display the poster from the inside of the book to introduce the March on Washington to students. Discuss the banner headline of the newspaper, as well as the other headlines on the page: *JFK Vows Push for More Jobs, Film and TV Stars to Consider Boycott of Jim Crow Places, Virginians Tell Why They Joined the Great D.C. Rally,* and so on. These articles show the divide between the rights of whites and blacks in 1963, and the issues about which civil rights leaders were concerned. (As an extension, look at other newspapers of the time and compare the front page coverage. How is it the same? different?)

2. Explain the lesson objectives to students, and review lesson vocabulary and background information.

3. Distribute the "Vast Sea of Humanity Raises Cry for 'Freedom'" handout (pages 9–12). Read and discuss the article with students.

4. Discuss the five W's and how and inverted pyramid journalistic writing styles. Have students complete the activity sheets (pages 13 and 14). Ask them to clip newspaper stories and identify how quickly the five W's and how questions are answered in their clippings.

5. Distribute and have students complete the "Civil Rights Who's Who" and "Unemployment and Income Comparison" activity sheets (pages 15 and 16). These activities will help students with comprehension.

Richmond Afro-American

Vast Sea Of Humanity Raises
Cry For 'Freedom'

241,000 join in fervent appeal to the Congress

By MARY STRATFORD
WASHINGTON

The cry was "freedom!"

The legions marched.

Some 241,000 singing, clapping, praying, marching Americans, Protestants, Jews, Catholics, black and white, flew, walked, rode, drove and roller skated to Washington Wednesday, to demand that a recalcitrant Congress pass effective civil rights legislation.

IT WAS the largest demonstration in the capital in the nation's history. Twenty-one chartered trains and 16 regular trains screamed along the rails into Union Station bringing 23,000 passengers.

Some 1,600 buses roared down the nation's highways bringing 60,000 passengers to Washington from as far west as Oklahoma City and Wyoming.

Over 30,000 marchers were from Philadelphia.

CLARKSDALE and Jackson, Mississippians, came in overalls, wearing them as a signal badge of honor. The marchers wore sandals, loafers, high heels, tennis shoes and Lena Horne walked in boots but the marching cadence was the same. The synchronized beat was "Freedom Now!"

THEY THRONGED from the gathering site at Washington Monument, along Constitution and Independence Aves., to the Lincoln Memorial.

At the foot of the brooding statue of Abraham Lincoln, they stood, sat on the grass, sat in chairs and hung from the trees.

It was a clear, golden day. Temperatures hovered about 87 degrees.

THE SKY WAS cloudless. A slight breeze stirred. An occasional bird fluttered by. A few airplanes droned in the sky. Helicopters bearing the press hung suspended overhead. One hundred thirty Congressmen spent 15 minutes with their constituents. Standing on the steps of the Lincoln Memorial facing the crowd, they heard the yells of "Pass the bill! Pass the bill!" The reference was to President Kennedy's proposed civil rights legislation.

The Congressmen left as A. Philip Randolph, director of the march, explained that the legislators could not remain because of legislation pending on the threatened railroad strike.

TWELVE OF THE nation's leaders, white and colored, addressed the thousands. Youthful John Lewis, chairman of the Student Non-Violent Coordinating committee, early expressed the mood of some of the multitude who cheered when he shouted.

"The time will come when will not confine our marching to Washington. We will march through the South, through the heart of Dixie, the way Sherman did but we will march with a spirit of dignity."

Though Randolph, father of the march, in an interview on the eve of the demonstration, told an AFRO reporter that the march was not to be a continuing movement, repeatedly, the leaders emphasized that the march was not to be considered a culmination of the civil rights movement, but the beginning.

THE REV. Martin Luther King, who received a standing ovation as he approached the microphones said, "1963 is not an end but a beginning. Those who hope that the colored citizens needed to blow off steam and will now be content have a rude awakening if the nation returns to business as usual."

WHITNEY M. YOUNG, JR., executive director of the National Urban League, declared, "This is a march just begun." He urged Congress to pass the necessary legislation, admit to the tragic injustice that has been done to the country and its colored citizens by discrimination and take intensive remedial steps to correct the damage.

JAMES FARMER, director of national CORE, chose to remain with 232 other freedom fighters in a Donaldsonville, La. jail and did not come to Washington but his message was read by Walter McKissick, CORE.

It is said, "We will not stop our militant, peaceful demonstrations. We will not come off the streets until we can work at any job befitting our skills any place in the land. . . . We will not stop til the dogs stop biting us in the South and the rats stop biting us in the North."

WALTER P. REUTHER, president of the International Union, UAW, asserted there are a lot of Americans who talk about brotherhood but who drop the "brother and keep the hood."

"This really should be the first step to mobilize the moral conscience of the nation," he added, calling on Congress to rise above partisan politics and enact legislation.

THE REV. EUGENE C. Blake, vice chairman of the Commission on Religion and Race, National Council of Churches, told the throng.

"As of August 28, 1963, we have achieved neither a non-segregated church nor a non-segregated society."

He deplored the churches' failure to put its own house in order and lamented, "We come to march behind and with those amazingly able leaders of the colored Americans, who, to the shame of almost every white American, have alone and without us, mirrored the suffering of the cross of Jesus Christ."

RABBI URI MILLER, president, Synagogue Council of America prayed: "Enable us to understand that our society—the American people—is one piece; that when any part of this society suffers, we all suffer. May we understand that he who discriminates is as morally hurt as is the one discriminated against, physically hurt."

MATHE WAHMANN, executive director of the National Catholic Conference for Interracial Justice said:

"We dedicate ourselves today to secure federal civil rights legislation which will guarantee every man a job based on his talents and training; legislation which will do away with the myth that the ownership of a public place of business carries any moral or legal right to reject a customer because of the color of his hair or of his skin."

"RABBI Joachim Prinz, president, American Jewish Congress, tracing the Jews own freedom struggles, declared that the most urgent problem is silence as pointed up by the silent onlookers during the Hitler regime in Germany.

"America must not become a nation of onlookers," he said. "It must not be silent. Not merely black America, but all of America. It must speak up and act, from the President down to the humblest of us, and not for the sake of the colored citizen but for the sake of America."

FIVE WOMEN were honored by the march committee. They were Mrs. Daisy Bates, Mrs. Diane Nash Bevel of the Student Non-Violent Coordinating Committee; Mrs. Herbert Lee, whose husband was killed in the civil rights struggle in the South two years ago; Mrs. Rosa Parks, whose refusal to give up her seat on the bus started the bus boycott in Montgomery, Ala.; Mrs. Gloria Richardson, veteran of Cambridge strife and Mrs. Medgar Evers, whose husband was slain in Jackson, Miss.

Mrs. Evers, who was an honoree at the Elks Convention in Boston, could not attend.

MORE THAN 11,000 policemen, national guardsmen, firemen and volunteers were detailed to the march.

The disturbances were few. Three white men were arrested. One was arrested when police found a loaded sawed-off shotgun on the seat of his car, the second was an American Nazi Party storm trooper who tried to make a speech and the third ran into the street and tore up the sign of one of the marchers.

OVER 1900 PERSONS were carried to area hospitals. Sixty of them were admitted. The others were re-[sic]. Two cases were suspected appendicitis.

As Randolph rose to address the thousands at the Lincoln Memorial, elsewhere in the city, six fire trucks were racing to a Government temporary building to put out a fire. It was a false alarm.

Two bomb reports were found to be baseless.

Food boxes to have been sold by the National Council of Churches were banned after two policemen who ate the lunches suffered suspected food poisoning. Improper refrigeration was blamed.

COMMISSIONER Walter Tobriner watched the proceedings on television at the District building. Afterwards, in a statement to the press, he congratulated the marchers, the organizations in back of the marchers, the police, and police reserves on the successful demonstration.

"No man is free unless all men are free. Never has a truism been more indelibly imprinted in the minds and hearts of the peoples of the world than through today's civil rights march."

THE MARCHERS began to gather at Washington Monument at about 6 a.m. Because of their sparse numbers, some segments of the press predicted the march would fail.

By 9:30 a.m., about 10,000 were on the grounds.

OSSIE DAVIS, playwright and actor, stood on a temporarily constructed platform and suggested that the marchers sit on the grass. Many of them did. One marcher remarked, "Coney Island was never like this."

JOAN BAEZ, folk singer, sang, "Oh Freedom." Davis, who emceed the program at the Washington Monument, asked for audience participation. Other entertainers had not arrived. Miss Dorothy Dale from Birmingham led several freedom songs.

Then, Odetta arrived.

"Roosevelt Johnson," Davis said. "Your child, Larry, is in the headquarters tent."

DAVIS ANNOUNCED, "At least 90,000 are here." The fear of failure left and a roar came from the assembly, as Davis went on, "We have had telephone calls from marchers who are on the way. If all of them get here, we will have 90,000 more."

The Elks presented $10,000 to the march committee. Carol Taylor, first colored airline hostess was introduced.

Josh White strummed his guitar and sang.

BAYARD RUSTIN, deputy director of the march, introduced Mrs. Daisy Bates and Mrs. Rosa Parks.

The death of W.E.B. DuBois in

Accra, Ghana was announced and the marchers stood in a moment in prayer.

The D.C. clergy marched carrying a casket borrowed from a local funeral home with the sign: "Jim Crow diehards. Filibuster is death rattles. The Rev. Martin Luther King, presiding."

MEANWHILE, leaders of the march, Randolph, Reuther, Lewis, Rabbi Miller, Young, Ahmann, Wilkins, Rabbi Prinz and the Rev. Mr. King were meeting with Congressional leaders on Capitol Hill.

At about 11:30 a.m., marchers began moving toward Lincoln Memorial. At about 1:10 p.m., at Lincoln Memorial, Ossie Davis introduced Odetta, who along with Camilla Williams, Peter, Paul and Mary, Josh White and the Freedom Singers, interpreted the march in song.

"Freedom riders ain't scared of no dogs.

"Freedom riders ain't scared of Barnett.

"I want my freedom."

THE REV. FRED Shuttlesworth from Birmingham shouted, "We are going to march together, groan together, pray together for freedom, freedom, freedom now."

JOSEPHINE BAKER was introduced, wearing a free French uniform. "This is the happiest day of my life. Today, you are together as salt and pepper, just as you should be. You are a united people at last."

THE REV. RALPH Abernathy asserted the march was the greatest demonstration since the signing of the emancipation.

Dr. Ralph Bunche: "My identification with this effort is automatic because I am colored but I would be here automatically as an American because what is being done today is one of the finest expressions of democracy."

DICK GREGORY, fresh from jail: "It is a pleasure to be here, nice to be out of jail. I never thought I would see the day that I would be asked for more fingerprints than autographs."

Burt Lancaster flew from Paris bringing a scroll with the names of 1,500 Americans in Paris who supported the march.

Harry Belafonte read a statement on behalf of a group of artists supporting the march.

Virginians arrived who had walked 250 miles. They were applauded.

THE NATIONAL anthem was led by Camilla Williams and invocation by the Rev. Patrick O'Boyle, archbishop of Washington.

Randolph's remarks were interrupted by the arrival of the Congressmen.

Music was interspersed throughout the program with Eva Jessey Choir and Miss Mahalia Jackson, participating. The crowd demanded an encore from Miss Jackson.

RANDOLPH exacted this promise from the thousands: "I pledge that I will join and support all actions undertaken in good faith in accord with the time-honored democratic tradition of non-violent protest, of peaceful assembly and petition, and of redress through the courts and the legislative process.

"I pledge to carry the message of the march to my friends and neighbors back home and to arouse them to an equal commitment and an equal effort.

"I will march and I will write letters. I will demonstrate and I will vote. I will work to make sure that my voice and those of my brothers ring clear and determined from every corner of our land.

"I pledge my heart and my mind and my body, unequivocally and without regard to personal sacrifice, to the achievement of social justice."

Name_____

Inverted Pyramid

Read the article "Vast Sea of Humanity Raises Cry for 'Freedom.'" Rewrite the story using the inverted pyramid format below. (Use both sides of the paper, if necessary.)

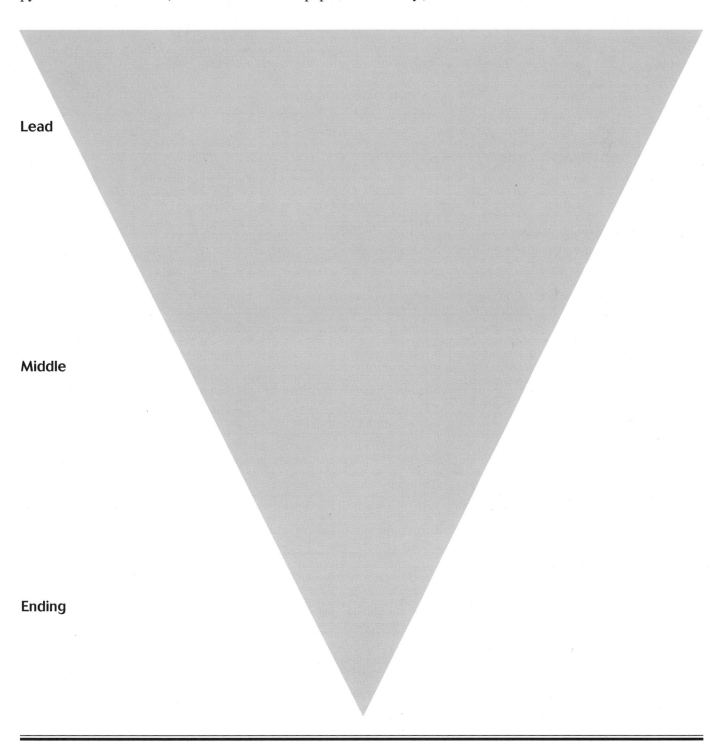

Lead

Middle

Ending

Name_____

The Five W's and How

The information in every good news story is basically the same: *Who* is the story about? *What* happened? *When* did it happen? *Where* did it happen? *Why* did it happen? *How* did it happen? Read the article "Vast Sea of Humanity Raises Cry for 'Freedom.'" Then answer the questions below.

Who?_____

_____

What?_____

_____

When?_____

_____

Where?_____

_____

Why?_____

_____

_____

How?_____

_____

_____

Name_____

Civil Rights Who's Who

Match each description with the appropriate person. Write the letter on the line. Some letters may be used more than once.

_____ 1. Mrs. Medgar Evers

_____ 2. Joan Baez

_____ 3. Rev. Eugene C. Blake

_____ 4. Ossie Davis

_____ 5. Mrs. Daisy Bates

_____ 6. Mrs. Gloria Richardson

_____ 7. Martin Luther King, Jr.

_____ 8. John Lewis

_____ 9. Rabbi Uri Miller

_____ 10. Rev. Patrick O'Boyle

_____ 11. Mathew Ahman

_____ 12. A. Philip Randolph

_____ 13. Walter P. Reuther

_____ 14. Bayard Rustin

_____ 15. Whitney M. Young, Jr.

_____ 16. James Farmer

_____ 17. Mrs. Diane Nash Bevel

_____ 18. Rabbi Joachim Prinz

_____ 19. Mrs. Rosa Parks

_____ 20. John F. Kennedy

A. Director of the March

B. Chairman, Student Non-Violent Coordinating Committee

C. President of the United States

D. Refused to give up her bus seat, triggering the bus boycott in Montgomery, Alabama

E. Director of National CORE

F. President of the International Union

G. Vice Chairman of the Commission on Religion and Race

H. Key March speaker and famous civil rights leader

I. President, Synagogue Council of America

J. Executive Director of the National Catholic Conference for Interracial Justice

K. Deputy Director of the March

L. President, American Jewish Congress

M. Playwright and actor

N. Folk singer

O. Archbishop of Washington

P. Her husband was a civil rights advocate, who was killed

Q. Executive Director of the National Urban League

R. Members of Student Non-Violent Coordinating Committee

S. Veteran of the Cambridge civil rights movement

Name_____

Unemployment and Income Comparison

Read the article "Vast Sea of Humanity Raises Cry for 'Freedom.'" Look at the tables below, comparing unemployment rates and income levels of blacks and whites in 1963. Then answer the following questions.

TABLE 1 Unemployment Rates: 1963

ALL CIVILIAN WORKERS			WHITE			BLACK AND OTHER NON-WHITES		
TOTAL	MALE	FEMALE	TOTAL	MALE	FEMALE	TOTAL	MALE	FEMALE
5.7	5.2	6.5	5.0	4.7	5.8	10.8	10.5	11.2

TABLE 2 Percent Distribution of Families by Race and Income Levels: 1963

PERCENT DISTRIBUTION BY INCOME LEVEL

Number	Under $3,000	$3,000 to $4,999	$5,000 to $6,999	$7,000 to $9,999	$10,000 to $11,999	$12,000 to $14,999	$15,000 and over
Total: 47,436	18.5	17.7	21.3	22.5	8.3	6.2	5.4
White: 42,663	15.8	17.0	21.8	23.8	9.0	6.6	5.9
Black*: 4,773	43.1	24.4	16.0	10.8	2.5	1.6	1.6

*This number includes blacks and other non-white heads of households.

1. Study Table 1, detailing unemployment rates in 1963. How do the unemployment numbers for whites compare to the unemployment numbers for blacks and other non-whites?

   _____

2. Study Table 2, showing the distribution of income. Compare the income levels between whites and blacks. What income level do most white families fall into? What income level do most black families fall into?

   _____

3. How do the income levels and unemployment rates relate to the March on Washington?

   _____

Extension Activities

1. Write a paragraph describing your opinion about the purpose of the March on Washington.

2. Write a paragraph explaining the significance of Carol Taylor's presence at the march.

A Speech by Martin Luther King, Jr.
"I Have a Dream"

Objective

• Understand the impact and significance of the speech

Vocabulary

Creed: A statement of principles; set of beliefs

Emancipation Proclamation: President Abraham Lincoln's declaration that freed all slaves in the territory at war with the Union. The proclamation was issued in September 1862, and became effective January 1, 1863.

Gentiles: Anyone not Jewish

Inalienable Rights: Rights belonging to a person by birth that cannot be taken away

Promissory Note: A promise in writing to pay a debt

Background

Dr. Martin Luther King, Jr. (1929–1968)

King was one of the most effective civil rights leaders of all time. He was born January 15, 1929, in Atlanta, Georgia, the son of a Baptist minister. King himself became a Baptist minister and came to preach at the same church as his father— Ebenezer Baptist Church. King became involved in the Montgomery bus boycott of 1955. His leadership and success gave him national prominence. In 1957, he founded the Southern Christian Leadership Conference to broaden the movement against segregation and discrimination. In the early 1960s, King organized protests to further awareness of discrimination against blacks. The protests were widely seen as an impetus for President Kennedy to submit a civil rights bill to Congress to prohibit racial discrimination in public places, and called for equality in employment and education. In 1964, Martin Luther King, Jr., was awarded the Nobel Peace Prize for his non-violent struggle during the early 1960s. King continued to speak out against racial injustice, poverty, and the Vietnam War until he was assassinated on April 4, 1968, by an escaped convict, James Earl Ray.

Suggested Lesson Plan

1. Explain the lesson objectives to students, and review lesson vocabulary and background information.

2. Distribute the "I Have a Dream" handout to students (pages 18–20). Read and discuss the speech with students. If possible, play a videotape recording of the speech (MPI Home Video, 1990, *The Speeches of Martin Luther King, Jr.: I Have a Dream!*). King's delivery gives the speech amazing passion and power, and has an impact beyond the written word.

3. Have students complete the "I Have a Dream" activity sheets (pages 21 and 22).

I Have a Dream

I am happy to join with you today in what will go down in history as the greatest demonstration for freedom in the history of our nation.

[1] Fivescore years ago, a great American, in whose symbolic shadow we stand today, signed the Emancipation Proclamation. This momentous decree came as a great beacon light of hope to millions of Negro slaves, who had been seared in the flames of withering injustice. It came as a joyous daybreak to end the long night of their captivity.

[2] But one hundred years later, the Negro is still not free; one hundred years later, the life of the Negro is still sadly crippled by the manacles of segregation and the chains of discrimination; one hundred years later, the Negro lives on a lonely island of poverty in the midst of a vast ocean of material prosperity; one hundred years later, the Negro is still languished in the corners of American society and finds himself in exile in his own land.

[3] So we've come here today to dramatize a shameful condition. In a sense we've come to our nation's capital to cash a check. When the architects of our republic

wrote the magnificent words of the Constitution and the Declaration of Independence, they were signing a promissory note to which every American was to fall heir. This note was a promise that all men, yes, black men as well as white men, would be guaranteed the unalienable rights of life, liberty, and the pursuit of happiness.

[4] It is obvious today that America has defaulted on the promissory note in so far as her citizens of color are concerned. Instead of honoring this sacred obligation, America has given the Negro people a bad check; a check which has come back marked "insufficient funds." We refuse to believe that the bank of justice is bankrupt. We refuse to believe that

there are insufficient funds in the great vaults of opportunity of this nation. And so we've come to cash this check, a check that will give us upon demand the riches of freedom and the security of justice.

[5] We have also come to this hallowed spot to remind America of the fierce urgency of now. This is no time to engage in the luxury of cooling off or to take the tranquilizing drug of gradualism. Now is the time to make real the promises of democracy; now is the time to rise from the dark and desolate valley of segregation to the sunlit path of racial justice; now is the time to lift our nation from the quicksands of racial injustice to the solid rock of brotherhood; now is the time to make justice a reality for all God's children. It would be fatal for the nation to overlook the urgency of the moment. This sweltering summer of the Negro's legitimate discontent will not pass until there is an invigorating autumn of freedom and equality.

[6] Nineteen sixty-three is not an end, but a beginning. And those who hope that the Negro needed to blow off steam and will now be content, will have a rude awakening if the Nation returns to

business as usual.

[7] There will be neither rest nor tranquility in America until the Negro is granted his citizenship rights. The whirlwinds of revolt will continue to shake the foundations of our nation until the bright day of justice emerges.

[8] But there is something that I must say to my people who stand on the warm threshold which leads into the palace of justice. In the process of gaining our rightful place we must not be guilty of wrongful deeds.

[9] Let us not seek to satisfy our thirst for freedom by drinking from the cup of bitterness and hatred. We must forever conduct our struggle on the high plane of dignity and discipline. We must not allow our creative protest to degenerate into physical violence. Again and again we must rise to the majestic heights of meeting physical force with soul force.

[10] The marvelous new militancy which has engulfed the Negro community must not lead us to a distrust of all white people, for many of our white brothers, as evidenced by their presence here today, have come to realize that their destiny is tied up with our destiny and they have come to realize that their freedom is inextricably bound to our freedom.

This offense we share mounted to storm the battlements of injustice must be carried forth by a biracial army. We cannot walk alone.

[11] And as we walk, we must make the pledge that we shall always march ahead. We cannot turn back. There are those who are asking the devotees of civil rights, "When will you be satisfied?" We can never be satisfied as long as the Negro is the victim of the unspeakable horrors of police brutality.

[12] We can never be satisfied as long as our bodies, heavy with the fatigue of travel, cannot gain lodging in the motels of the highways and the hotels of the cities. We cannot be satisfied as long as the Negro's basic mobility is from a smaller ghetto to a larger one.

[13] We can never be satisfied as long as our children are stripped of their selfhood and robbed of their dignity by signs stating "for whites only." We cannot be satisfied as long as a Negro in Mississippi cannot vote and a Negro in New York believes he has nothing for which to vote. No, we are not satisfied, and we will not be satisfied until justice rolls down like waters and righteousness like a mighty stream.

[14] I am not unmindful that

some of you come here out of excessive trials and tribulation. Some of you have come fresh from narrow jail cells. Some of you have come from areas where your quest for freedom left you battered by storms of persecution and staggered by the winds of police brutality. You have been the veterans of creative suffering. Continue to work with the faith that unearned suffering is redemptive.

[15] Go back to Mississippi; go back to Alabama; go back to South Carolina; go back to Georgia; go back to Louisiana; go back to the slums and ghettos of the northern cities, knowing that somehow this situation can, and will be changed. Let us not wallow in the valley of despair.

[16] So I say to you, my friends, that even though we must face the difficulties of today and tomorrow, I still have a dream. It is a dream deeply rooted in the American dream that one day this nation will rise up and live out the true meaning of its creed—we hold these truths to be self-evident, that all men are created equal.

[17] I have a dream that one day out in the red hills of Georgia, sons of former slaves and sons of former slave-owners will be able to sit down together at the table of brotherhood.

[18] I have a dream that one day, even the state of Mississippi, a state sweltering with the heat of injustice, sweltering in the heat of oppression, will be transformed into an oasis of freedom and justice.

[19] I have a dream that my four little children will one day live in a nation where they will not be judged by the color of their skin but by the content of their character. I have a dream today!

[20] I have a dream that one day, down in Alabama, with its vicious racists, with its governor having his lips dripping with the words of interposition and nullification, that one day, right down in Alabama, little black boys and black girls will be able to join hands with little white boys and white girls as sisters and brothers. I have a dream today!

[21] I have a dream that one day every valley shall be exalted, every hill and mountain shall be made low, the rough places shall be made plain, and the crooked places shall be made straight and the glory of the Lord will be revealed and all flesh shall see it together.

[22] This is our hope. This is the faith that I go back to the South with.

[23] With this faith we will be able to hew out the mountain of despair a stone of hope. With this faith we will be able to transform the jangling discords of our nation into a beautiful symphony of brotherhood.

[24] With this faith we will be able to work together, to pray together, to struggle together, to go to jail together, to stand up for freedom together, knowing that we will be free one day. This will be the day when all of God's children will be able to sing with new meaning—"My country 'tis of thee; sweet land of liberty; of thee I sing; land where my fathers died, land of the pilgrim's pride; from every mountainside, let freedom ring"—and if America is to be a great nation, this must become true.

[25] So let freedom ring from the prodigious hilltops of New Hampshire.

Let freedom ring from the mighty mountains of New York.

Let freedom ring from the heightening Alleghenies of Pennsylvania.

Let freedom ring from the snow-capped Rockies of Colorado.

Let freedom ring from the curvaceous slopes of California.

But not only that.

Let freedom ring from the Stone Mountain of Georgia.

Let freedom ring from Lookout Mountain of Tennessee.

Let freedom ring from every hill and molehill of Mississippi, from every mountainside, let freedom ring.

[26] When we allow freedom to ring, when we let it ring from every village and hamlet, from every state and city, we will be able to speed up that day when all of God's children—black men and white men, Jews and Gentiles, Catholics and Protestants—will be able to join hands and sing in the words of the old Negro spiritual, "Free at last, free at last; thank God Almighty, we are free at last!"

Reprinted with permission.

Name_____

I Have a Dream

1. On what occasion did Martin Luther King, Jr., give his "I Have a Dream" speech?

   _____

2. How long is fivescore?

   _____

3. King makes reference to "searing injustice." To what does this refer?

   _____

   _____

4. Who is the great American King refers to, in whose symbolic shadow we stand today?

   _____

5. What does "symbolic shadow" mean?

   _____

   _____

6. In paragraph 3, for what reason does King say the marchers have come together?

   _____

7. In paragraph 3, what does King say is the "promissory note"?

   _____

8. To what does the imagery of "manacles of segregation" and "chains of discrimination" refer? (Hint: Manacles usually refer to handcuffs.)

   _____

9. To which states does King refer most often? Why do you think he does this?

   _____

   _____

I Have a Dream (cont.)

10. In paragraph 5, how does King use repetition to make his point? What point does he make?

   _____

   _____

11. In paragraphs 5–7, what does King say will be a consequence of not acting?

   _____

12. In paragraph 9, King sets out the principles of the protest. What are they?

   _____

13. In paragraphs 11–13, King talks about what will satisfy the marchers. List six areas King wants changed before the marchers will be satisfied.

   _____

   _____

14. In paragraph 16, what is America's creed? From where does this creed come?

   _____

15. In paragraph 21, what does King mean when he says ". . . every valley shall be exalted, every hill and mountain shall be made low, the rough places shall be made plain, and the crooked places shall be made straight . . ."?

   _____

16. In paragraphs 23–26, in what three ways does King use the language of music to express his message?

   _____

   _____

17. In paragraph 26, how does King use opposites to make a point?

   _____

18. In the years that followed the March on Washington and King's great speech, three major pieces of civil rights legislation were passed: the Civil Rights Act of 1964, which bars racial discrimination in public places and requires equal employment opportunities; the Voting Rights Act of 1965, which bans all tests, literacy and others, from stopping people from voting; and the Civil Rights Act of 1968, which bans housing discrimination. Where does King allude to these three acts in his speech?

   _____

Editorial Cartoons

Objectives
- Understand pictorial symbolism used in editorial cartoons
- Recognize the use of humor and stereotypes in editorial cartoons
- Identify and judge a cartoonist's message and point of view

Vocabulary

Caricature: A drawing of a person with exaggerated features

Editorial Cartoon: A drawing, often with a caption, that illustrates an opinion on a current issue

Satyagraha: The theory of non-violent revolt that Mahatma Gandhi used to lead the Indians against British rule and acquired freedom for India in 1948

Symbolism: In editorial cartoons, art (symbol) is used to illustrate or represent (symbolize) an idea, person, country, and so on.

Background

Cartoonists convey their opinions using art rather than words. Even though most editorial cartoons contain some text—usually just a caption—most of the message is found in the art. The cartoonist expects the reader to understand the message conveyed in the illustration. The cartoonist must use familiar symbols and caricatures to relate his or her message about the event being editorialized.

Suggested Lesson Plan

1. Explain the lesson objectives to students, and review lesson vocabulary and background information. Explain that editorial cartoons are opinions, just like written editorials, only they are expressed through illustration.
2. Have students complete the editorial cartoon activity sheets (pages 24–26). Invite students to study each cartoon, thinking about how each relates to and expresses an opinion about the March on Washington and the civil rights movement.
3. Have students draw their own editorial cartoons to express their opinions about the March on Washington or an issue or event currently in the news.
4. To demonstrate that editorial cartoons are actually illustrated opinions, invite students to put into words the opinions or viewpoints expressed in the illustrations.

Name_____

"... That's the Spirit!"

This cartoon appeared in the *Atlanta Constitution* on Wednesday, August 28, 1963. Study the cartoon and complete each statement by writing the correct letter on the line.

1. _____ The man hovering over the marchers in the cartoon is:

   a. Martin Luther King, Jr.
   b. Mahatma Gandhi
   c. John F. Kennedy
   d. Rev. Ralph Abernathy

2. _____ The man hovering over the marchers in the cartoon represents:

   a. the spirit of Christmas past
   b. the spirit of non-violent protest
   c. the spirit of George Washington
   d. all of the above

3. _____ The people in the cartoon are:

   a. protesting the Beatles tour of America
   b. marching for lower taxes
   c. protesting for universal civil rights
   d. none of the above

4. _____ The people in the cartoon are:

   a. carrying placards with protest slogans
   b. marching to bring awareness to their issues
   c. focusing attention on the civil rights movement
   d. all of the above

5. _____ The editorial cartoon uses:

   a. symbolism to make its point
   b. satire to make its point
   c. ridicule to make its point
   d. none of the above

6. What clues tell readers where the activity in the cartoon takes place?

   _____

. . . That's the Spirit!"

Extension Activity

Explain how the cartoon relates to the "I Have a Dream" speech of Martin Luther King, Jr.

Name_____

"Lending a Badly Needed Helping Hand"

This cartoon first appeared in the *Richmond Afro-American* on September 7, 1963. Study the cartoon and complete each statement by writing the correct letter on the line.

1. _____ The hand in the cartoon represents:

   a. Martin Luther King, Jr.
   b. the marchers who went to Washington, D.C.
   c. supporters of civil rights
   d. all of the above

2. _____ The older man in the cartoon represents:

   a. the United States Senate
   b. the United States House of Representatives
   c. the United States Congress
   d. none of the above

3. _____ The cartoonist uses caricature to portray:

   a. the marchers
   b. members of Congress
   c. elderly people
   d. none of the above

4. _____ According to the cartoon, the cartoonist is concerned about:

   a. civil rights legislation
   b. the pace of the passage of civil rights legislation
   c. the age of the man in the hat
   d. all of the above

5. _____ According to the cartoon, the "helping hands" are:

   a. the people who went to Washington, D.C.
   b. United States Senators
   c. United States House of Representatives
   d. none of the above

Lending A Badly Needed Helping Hand

Extension Activity

Explain how this editorial cartoon, specifically the title, relates to the march on Washington.

Name_____

"Sorry, But You Have an Incurable Skin Condition"

This cartoon first appeared in the *Washington Post* on July 4, 1963. Study the cartoon and complete each statement by writing the correct letter on the line.

1. _____ The two men standing in the cartoon are:

   a. doctors examining a patient

   b. doctors interviewing another doctor for a job

   c. eye doctors checking a patient's eyes

   d. none of the above

2. _____ The name of the hospital the two doctors work for indicates that the hospital:

   a. only hires white doctors

   b. has race-based hiring practices

   c. is the Lily White Hospital

   d. all of the above

3. _____ The man in the chair:

   a. is a doctor

   b. is a patient getting a check-up

   c. is selling medical supplies

   d. none of the above

4. _____ The man in the chair:

   a. is applying for a job

   b. has a disease

   c. came in for a check-up

   d. none of the above

5. _____ According to the cartoon, what skin condition does the sitting man have?

   a. an allergic rash

   b. a sunburn

   c. eczema

   d. his skin color is black

6. Explain the message of this cartoon.

   _____

   _____

"SORRY, BUT YOU HAVE AN INCURABLE SKIN CONDITION"

Literature Connection
"The Battle Hymn of the Republic"
"Free at Last"

Objectives

• Understand songs as primary source material
• Interpret symbolism used in songs

Vocabulary

Conjurer: Sorcerer

Contemners: To scorn or have contempt

Transfigure: To change and to glorify

Background

"Free at Last" and "The Battle Hymn of the Republic" were popular anthems in African Americans' struggle for freedom. "The Battle Hymn of the Republic" was sung at the March on Washington, and Martin Luther King, Jr., quoted lines from the song "Free at Last" as he ended his rousing keynote address to a crowd that had swelled to over 240,000.

The origin of "The Battle Hymn of the Republic" is well known. It was written by Julia Ward Howe in the winter of 1861. Howe wrote the poem while looking out her window in the Willard Hotel in Washington, D.C., at army campfires flickering in the distance. The melody was a favorite tune called "John Brown's Body." Her song soon became a favorite marching song in the North by Union soldiers during the Civil War. It was first published by *Atlantic Monthly* in February 1862.

The origin of "Free at Last" is less certain. It probably originated as a black spiritual, because the syncopation of the song was common in the rhythms of these spirituals. The song was probably sung during the Civil War, though this is not certain, because it wasn't published until the end of the 19th century.

Suggested Lesson Plan

1. Distribute "The Battle Hymn of the Republic" and "Free at Last" handouts (pages 28 and 29). If possible, play these songs for students, and sing them. Recordings of "The Battle Hymn of the Republic" are fairly easy to come by. The music is stirring, forceful, and defiant.

2. Distribute the "Songs of Struggle and Triumph" activity sheet (page 30). Ask students to carefully read and think about the meaning and feeling behind the song lyrics before answering the questions.

The Battle Hymn of the Republic

Mine eyes have seen the glory of the coming of the Lord;
He is trampling out the vintage where the grapes of wrath are stored;
He hath loos'd the fateful lightning of His terrible swift sword,
His truth is marching on.

Chorus
Glory, glory hallelujah!
Glory, glory hallelujah!
Glory, glory hallelujah!
His truth is marching on.

I have seen Him in the watch fires of a hundred circling camps;
They have builded Him an altar in the ev'ning dews and damps;
I can read His righteous sentence by the dim and flaring lamps,
His day is marching on.
Chorus

I have read a fiery gospel writ in burnish'd rows of steel:
"As ye deal with My contemners, so with you My grace shall deal";
Let the Hero born of woman crush the serpent with His heel,
Since God is marching on.
Chorus

He has sounded forth the trumpet that shall never call retreat;
He is sifting out the hearts of men before His judgment seat.
Oh, be swift, my soul, to answer Him! Be jubilant my feet!
Our God is marching on.
Chorus

In the beauty of the lilies Christ was born across the sea,
With a glory in His bosom that transfigures you and me;
As He died to make men holy let us die to make men free,
While God is marching on.
Chorus

Free at Last

Chorus
Free at last, free at last.,
I thank God I'm free at last.
Free at last, free at last.;
I thank God I'm free at last.

Satan is mad and I am glad,
I thank God I'm free at last;
He missed the soul he thought he had,
I thank God I'm free at last. Oh,
Chorus

Satan is like a snake in the grass,
I thank God I'm free at last;
He's always in some Christian's path,
I thank God I'm free at last. Oh,
Chorus

Satan is a liar and a conjurer too,
I thank God I'm free at last;
If you don't mind he'll conjure you,
I thank God I'm free at last. Oh,
Chorus

I know Satan and I know him well,
I thank God I'm free at last;
I whipped him down at the gates of hell,
I thank God I'm free at last. Oh,
Chorus

Name_____

Songs of Struggle and Triumph

"The Battle Hymn of the Republic"

1. Why would organizers of the March on Washington sing this Civil War song?

   _____

2. In his speech, Martin Luther King, Jr., said, "As we walk, we must make the pledge that we shall always march ahead." How is that sentiment stated in the song?

   _____

3. Why is this song appropriate for both the civil rights movement and the struggle for freedom during the Civil War?

   _____

4. In verse 5, how committed are the people fighting for freedom?

   _____

5. If this song can be viewed as a metaphor for the civil rights struggle, to what could the serpent in verse 3 refer?

   _____

"Free at Last"

6. What is the overwhelming cry of the song "Free at Last"?

   _____

7. In the civil rights movement, for whom or what is Satan a metaphor?

   _____

8. How do these songs reflect the spiritual component of the civil rights movement and its leaders?

   _____

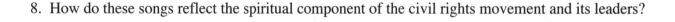

Answers

The Five Ws and How (page 14)

Who: 241,000 Americans, black and white, of all faiths

What: Marched on Washington

When: August 28, 1963

Where: They gathered at the Washington Monument, along Constitution and Independence Aves., to the Lincoln Memorial.

Why: To highlight the need for Congress to pass civil rights legislation

How: They came by foot, train, bus, car, skates, and airplane.

Civil Rights Who's Who (page 15)

1. P, 2. N, 3. G, 4. M, 5. R, 6. S, 7. H, 8. B, 9. I, 10. O, 11. J, 12. A, 13. F, 14. K, 15. Q, 16. E, 17. R, 18. L, 19. D, 20. C

Unemployment and Income Comparison (page 16)

1. Black unemployment was 10.8, almost two times the white unemployment rate of 5.0.

2. The highest number of white families fell into the $7,000 to $9,999 income bracket; the highest number of black families fell into the under $3,000 income bracket, less than half the income than the average white family.

3. The marchers were marching for economic opportunity. It is clear from the statistics in these charts that blacks were being denied equal job opportunities.

Extension Activity:

1. Paragraphs will vary.

2. Carol Taylor was the first African American flight attendant. The marchers were protesting for civil rights so that blacks could have equal employment opportunities.

I Have a Dream (pages 21 and 22)

1. The March on Washington

2. A score is 20 years; "fivescore" is 100 years.

3. Slavery

4. Abraham Lincoln, 16th President of the United States

5. The great statue of Lincoln; the statue is a symbol of Lincoln

6. To dramatize a "shameful condition"

7. The Declaration of Independence, which promised life, liberty, and the pursuit of happiness

8. The imagery of slavery

9. Mississippi, 4; Georgia, 3; Alabama, 3; New York, 2; South Carolina, Louisiana, New Hampshire, Pennsylvania, Colorado, California, Tennessee, 1. In 1963, most protests took place in the South because this is where most of the restrictive segregation laws were enforced, including Jim Crow and poll laws.

10. The word *now* is repeated to emphasize that black Americans have waited long enough.

11. Revolt will continue to shake the country.

12. Meet the struggle with dignity, discipline, and non-violence

13. An end to police brutality, access to lodging, freedom of movement, an end to "whites only" segregation, suffrage, and having a real reason to vote

14. "All men are created equal," from the Declaration of Independence

15. This is a metaphor for making all people equal, no matter what their station is in life.

16. King references the symphony of brotherhood and then quotes from two songs: "My Country 'Tis of Thee" and "Free at Last."

17. By contrasting people who historically have had differing opinions, he calls on all people to come together.

18. The Civil Rights Act of 1964 (paragraphs 4, 5, and 7); The Voting Rights Act of 1965 (paragraph 13); The Civil Rights Act of 1968 (paragraph 12).

". . . That's the Spirit!" (page 24)

1. B, 2. B, 3. C, 4. D, 5. A,

6. The Washington Monument in the background is a visual clue that the protest march is in Washington, D.C.

"Lending a Badly Needed Helping Hand" (page 25)

1. B, 2. C, 3. B, 4. B, 5. A,

Extension Activity: Answers will vary but may include: That the March was providing leadership to the Congress.

"Sorry, But You Have an Incurable Skin Condition" (page 26)

1. B, 2. D, 3. A, 4. A, 5. D,

6. Hiring practices in America that excluded qualified people from getting jobs is wrong and should be made unlawful.

Songs of Struggle and Triumph (page 30)

1. Abolitionists and Union soldiers fighting for the end of slavery sang this song. The song was also sung during the fight to pass civil rights legislation and to put an end to racial inequality and discrimination.

2. In at least two ways: the refrains "His truth is marching on," "His day is marching on," "Since God is marching on," "Our God is marching on," "While God is marching on"; and the 4th verse "He has sounded forth the trumpet that shall never call retreat."

3. Answers will vary, but may include that both are struggles for freedom: freedom from the chains of slavery in the Civil War, freedom from the chains of the economic oppression of prejudice in the civil rights movement.

4. They are willing to die for the cause.

5. Slavery in the Civil War; prejudice in the civil rights movement

6. "Free at Last" emphasizes the longing cry for freedom. It is repeated eight times in the song, and six times in the chorus.

7. Prejudice and racial inequality

8. Faith carries people through the struggle. Both songs have God as the focus: "The Battle Hymn" talks about God's strength and righteousness. "Free at Last" thanks God for freedom.

31

Teacher Resources

Banks, James A. and Cherry A. *March Toward Freedom: A History of Black Americans*. David S. Lake Publishers: Belmont, California, 1978.

Lewis, David Levering. *King: A Biography*. University of Illinois Press: Urbana, Illinois, 1970.

Lischer, Richard. *The Preacher King: Martin Luther King, Jr. and the Words That Moved America*. Oxford University Press: New York, 1995.

Miller, William Robert. *Martin Luther King, Jr.: His Life, Martyrdom, and Meaning for the World*. Weybright and Tally: New York, 1968.

Schulke, Flip, editor. *Martin Luther King, Jr.: A Documentary . . . Montgomery to Memphis*. W. W. Norton & Company: New York, 1976.

Schwartz, Bernard, editor. *Statutory History of the United States Civil Rights, Part II*. Chelsea House: New York, 1970.

Washington, James Melvin, editor. *I Have a Dream: Writings and Speeches That Changed the World*. HarperCollins Publishers: New York, 1992.

Wattenberg, Ben. J. *The Statistical History of the United States: From Colonial Times to the Present*. Basic Book, Inc., Publishers: New York, 1976.

Witherspoon, Wm. Roger. *Martin Luther King, Jr. . . . To the Mountaintop*. Doubleday & Company, Inc.: Garden City, New York, 1985.

Student Resources

Adler, David A. *Martin Luther King, Jr.: Free at Last*. Holiday House: New York,

Darby, Jean. *Martin Luther King, Jr.* Lerner Publications Company: Minneapolis, Minnesota, 1990.

Haskins, Jim. *I Have a Dream: The Life and Words of Martin Luther King, Jr.* Millbrook Press: Brookfield, Connecticut, 1992.

Patterson, Lillie. *Martin Luther King, Jr. and the Freedom Movement*. Facts on File: New York, 1989.